ETHEL'S PERFECT DAY

Maite Butron & Brady Ough
Illustrated by Rafael Butron

Ethel Publications
Australia
Copyright © 2019 by Maite Butron & Brady Ough
Illustrations Copyright © 2019 by Rafael Butron

Written by
Maite Butron & Brady Ough

Illustrated by Rafael Butron

Edited by Morgana Willing

ISBN 978-0-6483126-4-2
ISBN 978-0-6483126-5-9   (ebook)

... INTRODUCTION

The Ethel the Echidna series are childrens' books with simple stories that gently show both personal and social boundaries encouraging the healthy development of children.

These stories introduce the practice of mindfulness, emphasizing the importance of awareness about choice when it comes to our behaviour.

Ethel
Jeremy.
Clive
Claudia

ETHEL'S PERFECT DAY

... A PARENTS' GUIDE

This story is about the limitations of perfectionism and resistance to change.

This is shown through Ethel's desire to have control over her environment and her relationships.

When Ethel has this control, she considers her day 'perfect'. However, upon discovering her friends getting together without her, Ethel experiences an overwhelming amount of emotions.

She makes assumptions about the situation and this causes her unnecessary pain. Ethel draws on internal resources — observing the changing patterns of the clouds - to gain the insights that change is a natural part of life and mistakes happen.

Ethel the echidna always woke up at the perfect time of sunrise.

On this fine morning it was 6.17 a.m.

For breakfast, Ethel made
herself a perfect bowl of
toasted beetle and cricket
muesli and a cup of her
famous lizard leg tea.

After cleaning up
until her sink sparkled
perfectly, Ethel went out
to her garden to water
her perfectly pretty
plants.

Ethel stretched and looked up at the bright blue sky and saw perfect fluffy, white clouds. They looked like sheep trotting across a great blue field.

"What a perfect day," Ethel smiled to herself.

Ethel popped on her
favourite spotted
gumboots and headed
off to the river for a
peaceful morning walk.

As she got closer to
the river, Ethel heard
music and laughter.
It was getting louder
and louder…

HAHA
HA
HA
HA
HA
HA
HA!
HA
HA
HA!
HA!

... Ethel peered from
behind a giant fig
tree and gasped
with shock and
horror.

HA HA!

Ethel saw her friends;
Jeremy, Claudia and
Clive having a party.

She clutched at her
heart, not sure if it was
still beating. Her friends
were having a party
without her!

That was when Clive spotted her. "Ah, Ethel, you're a bit late. The invitation said to arrive at 7:00 a.m. sharp."

"I never got an invitation," said Ethel crossly. Tears began to well in her eyes, and she turned to stomp off. Ethel's perfect day was ruined.

Jeremy stood in front of
Ethel and simply raised
his eyebrows.

"Clive hates me," bawled
Ethel. "He wouldn't lend
me his pot plant, he
never eats my triple bug
brownies, and now he
forgot to invite me to his
party."

Ethel sobbed a bit more
and said, "I just want to
be a perfect friend and
a perfect echidna."

Jeremy smiled and said,
"Clive doesn't hate you
Ethel, he just made a
mistake and forgot to
invite you to his party. It
doesn't mean you're a
bad echidna."

Ethel just looked up at the sky thinking about what Jeremy had said. She smiled. The clouds had now changed from sheep to a frog, a fish and two little ponies.

Ethel pondered out loud, "it does make more sense that Clive just made a simple mistake. Perhaps even I can make mistakes sometimes."

Ethel turned to Jeremy and giggled, "maybe a day can still be perfect even if mistakes are made."

Jeremy grinned; he could see
that Ethel felt much better.
"Come on Ethel," he said, "let's
have some of Clive's yummy
slug soup."

ETHEL'S
PERFECT
DAY

Clive's Slug Soup

I don't cook many things, but if there is one thing I love its slugs. Fat ones, skinny ones, long ones and short ones. I'm not fussed on their colour, I just love slugs. This is a simple recipe my mother made; and her mother made it before her. And her mother made it before her, and so on dating back many a year.

Ingredients:
1 Bucket assorted slugs
1/2 A bucket oak root- chopped
5 Rosemary nettles
4 Carrots- chopped
2 Bulbs garlic- peeled
5 Onions- peeled and chopped
6 Large potatoes- peeled and chopped
5 Claws-full of salt

Method:

1. Cover the slugs with two buckets of water and soak overnight.
2. Drain the water off the slugs and rinse with another bucket of water.
3. Scatter the slugs over two roasting trays and bake in the oven until the slugs start to brown.
4. Add the slugs to a large soup pot and cover with 4 buckets of water.
5. Add all other ingredients and put three logs under the pot and stoke the fire.
6. Stir the pot every three hours with a clean oak branch and add another log to the fire. Continue until three nights have passed and all the vegetables and slugs have turned to mush.

I would like to mention that I love slugs and this soup puts all other slug recipes to shame. Serve to your most special friends and family.

With kindest regards,
Clive.

Beetle and Cricket Muesli

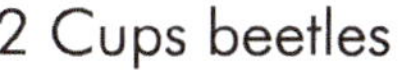

2 Cups beetles
2 Cups crickets
3 Cups shaved oak tree root
2 Claws-full of blossom honey

Method:

When the sun is high in the sky and no clouds can be seen or smelt, sprinkle the beetles and crickets over a flat rock and drizzle with honey. Take a nap and then watch the sky to see it turn from blue to pink. Stomp over the mixture four times wearing clean iron boots. Store in an airtight clay pot all ready for breakfast.

This story was written by Brady Ough.
He is a parent, grandparent, chef, massage
therapist and energetic healer.

Concept and parenting guide by Maite Butron.
She is a parent and grandparent who works as
a Holistic Counsellor, Relationship Counsellor
and Life Coach.

Both authors are passionate about boundaries
and active, respectful parenting.

Original watercolour drawings by
Rafael Butron, artist and parent.

Edited by Morgana Willing, parent and
early childhood educator.

Recipe inspirations and fun add-ons by
Sofia Hartley.

Design by BA&D.

Eternal gratitude to Ben Jarvis, for
his intellectual and legal guidance.